25 Ultimate experiences

Africa

Make the most of your time on Earth

ROUGH GUIDES

25 YEARS 1982–2007

NEW YORK • LONDON • DELHI

Contents

Introduction

EXPERIENCES have always been at the heart of the Rough Guide concept. A group of us began writing the books **25 years ago** (hence this celebratory mini series) and wanted to share the kind of travels we had been doing ourselves. It seems bizarre to recall that in the early 1980s, travel was very much a minority pursuit. Sure, there was a lot of tourism around, and that was reflected in the guidebooks in print, which traipsed around the established sights with scarcely a backward look at the local population and their life. We wanted to change all that: to put a country or a city's popular culture centre stage, to highlight the clubs where you could hear local music, drink with people you hadn't come on holiday with, watch the local football, join in with the festivals. And of course we wanted to push travel a bit further, inspire readers with the confidence and knowledge to break away from established routes, to find pleasure and excitement in remote islands, or desert routes, or mountain treks, or in street culture.

Twenty-five years on, that thinking seems pretty obvious: we all want to experience something real about a destination, and to seek out travel's **ultimate experiences**. Which is exactly where these **25 books** come in. They are not in any sense a new series of guidebooks. We're happy with the series that we already have in print. Instead, the **25s** are a collection of ideas, enthusiasms and inspirations: a selection of the very best things to see or do – and not just before you die, but now. Each selection is gold dust. That's the brief to our writers: there is no room here for the average, no space fillers. Pick any one of our selections and you will enrich your travelling life.

But first of all, take the time to browse. Grab a half dozen of these books and let the ideas percolate ... and then begin making your plans.

Mark Ellingham

Founder & Series Editor, Rough Guides

Ultimate experiences
Africa

01 MESSING *about in*

This really is perfect peace, you think to yourself, as your *mokoro* pilot's paddle dips softly into the glossy water. *Mokoros* are traditional canoes, paddled from the back like a punt, with room for one or two sitting in front. They're by far the most relaxing way to explore the wildlife-rich backwaters of the Okavango, the only major African river which doesn't make it to the ocean: thanks to freak tectonic movements in prehistoric times, the Okavango ends up being sucked dry in the Kalahari desert.

The river rises in the mountains of Angola, where the October and November rains send high waters cascading southward. These waters eventually meander across the plains of northern Botswana where, from June to October, they flood a huge inland delta of channels and lagoons. The result is a unique seasonal habitat which harbours elephants and hippos, soggy-hoofed red lechwe and sitatunga antelopes, and (it's said) six-metre-long crocodiles.

the OKAVANGO DELTA

Mokoros used to be made from hollowed-out tree trunks, but these days the Botswanans prefer fibreglass – less picturesque, but arguably more practical. Riding around in one places you so low on the sparkling water that you can trace around floating leaves with your fingers and find yourself eye-to-eye with herons and wattled cranes. You may also spot malachite kingfishers, shining like jewels from papyrus perches, and frogs squatting on lily pads like fairy-tale princes, just waiting to be kissed.

need to know

Many of the safari lodges in the Okavango Delta include *mokoro* excursions in their room rate. You can independently arrange day-trips and longer camping excursions with safari operators in the delta's main gateway town, Maun, which is served by flights from many southern African cities. The best time to come is July to September, dry season in the delta, by which time the previous year's rainfall in Angola has brought the floods to a peak.

2 HOT-AIR ballooning over the Maasai Mara

The Maasai Mara is Kenya's slab of the Serengeti, a succulent, acacia-dotted grassland that's home to some of the densest concentrations of wildlife in Africa. This is where the BBC films "Big Cat Diary", and where wildebeest by the thousand swarm across the crocodile-jammed Mara river. Animals hold such dazzling sway here you feel as if you've landed in the natural world's answer to New York.

But if you need to get away from even this, take a balloon flight over the reserve: every vivid second will stay with you for the rest of your life. You'll be woken at 5am, in the pitch-dark chill of the savanna pre-dawn, and driven to the river bank, where a boat takes you across to the launching site. As the doves start their dawn chorus and the sun's rays sneak through the woods, the huge Mongolfier is inflated. With little ceremony, you climb in and, a few hot blasts later, begin to rise through the trees. There's almost no sound apart from that occasional whoosh, and nothing to detract from the exquisite sensation of floating in space, the soft brush of the breeze on your cheek, and animals in every direction.

Just below, vultures wheel from treetop roosts. The chocolate-brown river reveals stirring hippos. Hyenas might be scrapping over a buffalo carcass, and you might notice jackals bravely rushing in for a nip of their share. An invisible lion vents a guttural roar, more like a huge belch. Zebra and wildebeest canter away from the balloon's advancing shadow. And a line of elephants emerges from the trees, adults ear-flapping, youngsters fooling at the sides. After it's all over, the slap-up breakfast and chilled sparkling wine you're served upon returning to terra firma almost seem unnecessary fripperies.

need to know

Balloon flights are offered by several of the larger safari camps and lodges; they'll come and pick you up if you're staying elsewhere in the Maasai Mara. Expect to pay around $400 per person.

03 **PONY-TREKKING** IN LESOTHO

Landlocked within South Africa, the mountain kingdom of Lesotho is a poor but magical place. A lot of the magic is encapsulated in those two words – mountain kingdom. Lesotho is one of Africa's few surviving monarchies, proud of its distinctive history, and the whole country lies above an altitude of 1000 metres, its highest peaks soaring into a distinctly un-African realm of mists and dank cloud. Back in the nineteenth century, the dominant figure in the country's history, King Moshoeshoe (pronounced Mo-shweh-shweh) I, acquired a pony stolen from a farm in the Cape. Its suitability for Lesotho's hilly terrain was soon clear, and the people, the Basotho, quickly became a nation of horse riders. They remain so today. Few of the scattered villages of the mountains are reached by any road, tarred or otherwise. Everywhere is connected by paths, and to get anywhere you need to walk or ride.

Pony trekking isn't really an "activity", something to do instead of canoeing or bird-watching; get atop a horse here and you're participating in Basotho life. There's nothing prim about it either; no one will comment on your posture or how you hold the reins, and given that the paths only go uphill or downhill, you'll do a lot more plodding than prancing. You'll greet passing locals, breathe mountain air, village woodsmoke and the scent of clammy horse sweat, and hear the ringing shouts of barefoot children rounding up goats on the hillside – accompanied, all the while, by the steady clip-clop of your sure-footed pony picking its way along the path.

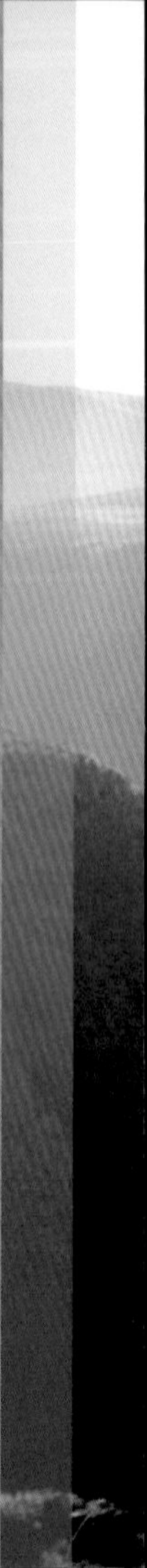

need to know

Pony treks can last a couple of hours or the best part of a week; riding experience isn't necessary. A good place to arrange them is Malealea Lodge (ⓦwww.malealea.co.ls), an hour's drive south of the capital Maseru, which is 500km south of Johannesburg. An overnight trek typically costs $45, with accommodation in a traditional round mud hut with a thatched roof. A share of the proceeds goes to pony and hut owners.

04 *Haggling* in the souks of Fes

Everywhere you look in Fes's Medina – the ancient walled part of the city – there are alleys bedecked with exquisite hand-made crafts. Here the city's distinctive ceramics jostle for space with rich fabrics, musical instruments and red tasselled fezzes (which take their name from the city). Most of these items are made in the Medina itself, in areas such as the carpenters' souk, redolent of cedarwood, or in the rather less aromatic tanneries, where leather is cured in stinky vats of, among other substances, cow's urine and pigeon poo. In the dyers' souk, the cobbles run with multicoloured pigments used to tint gaudy hanks of wool, while nearby Place Seffarine, by the tenth-century Kairaouine Mosque, reverberates to the sound of metalworkers hammering intricate designs into brass.

Should you wish to buy, however, it's not a matter of "how much?", "here you go", "bye". Love it or hate it, haggling is de rigueur. These crafts are made with love and patience, and should not be bought in a rush. Rather, the shopkeeper will expect you to dally awhile, perhaps enjoy a cup of tea – sweet, green and flavoured with Moroccan mint – and come to an agreement on a price. This is both a commercial transaction and a game, and skilled hagglers are adept at theatrics – "How much? Are you crazy?" "For this fine piece of art? Don't insult me!"

Know how much you are prepared to pay, offer something less, and let the seller argue you up. If you don't agree a price, nothing is lost, and you've spent a pleasant time conversing with the shopkeeper. And you can always go back the next day and reopen discussions.

need to know

There are a few flights into Fes, but it's usually easier to fly into Casablanca and take a train from there. Spring and autumn are the best times to visit. The upmarket places to stay are mostly in the Ville Nouvelle, a taxi ride or long walk from the Medina, but there's a cluster of budget accommodation around Bab Boujeloud, where the Medina begins.

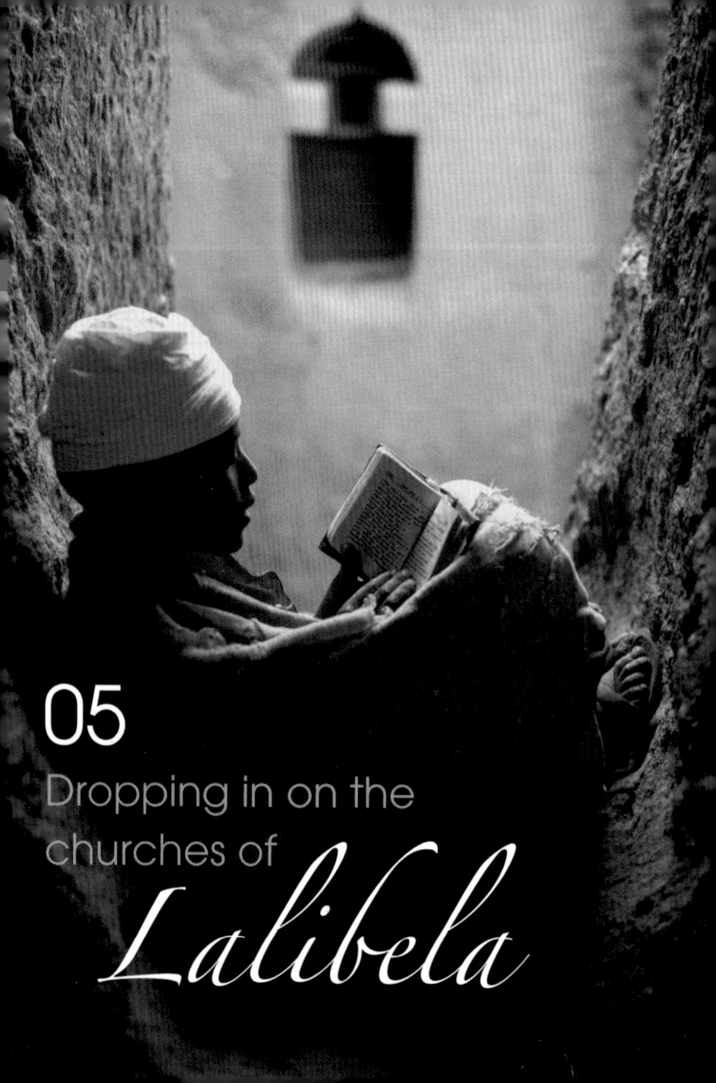

05

Dropping in on the churches of *Lalibela*

Lalibela, in Ethiopia's highlands, is so rural that it doesn't even have a bank. Yet in the thirteenth century it was capital of the Zagwe dynasty, one of whose last rulers, King Lalibela, embarked on a quest to build a Holy Land on Ethiopian soil.

Historians say he was inspired to build the town's famous rock-hewn churches after a pilgrimage to Jerusalem, while the devout claim that he was instructed by angels during a poison-induced sleep. Whatever the real reason, the town of Lalibela, built as a "new Jerusalem", leaves pilgrims and visitors alike humbled by the elegance of its churches. Gracing a rocky plateau and intricately carved, they mostly lie in two interconnected groups scattered along the "Jordan River", another biblical landscape feature that King Lalibela designed.

This major UNESCO World Heritage Site is hidden from view until you are literally upon it – a strategic choice, offering protection from marauders. All the churches are monolithic structures, dug deep down into the rock. As you pass through carved gullies leading from one church to the next, you can look in on caves containing the skeletons of deceased monks, or gaze up to cubby holes in the red rock face to see yellow-robed pilgrims reciting the Bible in Ge'ez, an archaic form of Amharic.

The churches remain vibrant centres of worship, their monks, nuns and priests fervently engaged with the Ethiopian Orthodox Church's demanding calendar of events. Every church has a hereditary guardian priest dedicated to this medieval world of incense, beeswax candles and ritual – though, incongruously, they all seem to keep a pair of sunglasses handy should you try a photograph using a flash.

need to know

Ethiopian Airlines has flights from Addis Ababa to Lalibela; driving there (a 4WD is essential) takes a full day from the capital. It's not advisable to visit in the rainy season (July–Sept), when roads become treacherous and even flights may be cancelled. A three-day pass covering all eleven churches costs around $18. Hiring a guide is worthwhile, at around $12 per day.

06 Clubbing in Dakar

"Nanga def?" "Jama rek." The throaty greeting and response of the Wolof language is all around as you hustle to get into a soirée at one of the busy clubs in Dakar, Senegal's dusty capital. Under the orange glow of street lamps, outrageously upfront flirting fills the warm, perfume-laden air like static.

Inside, the lights swirl; the simple stage fills; the clear high tones of the lead vocals surge through a battering of talking drums; and the floor becomes a mass of shaking hips, tummies, arms and legs. It's no place to be shy – but there's no better place in Africa to get over shyness quickly.

Nightlife in Dakar is dominated by big-name musicians and their clubs. The city, staunchly Muslim (most Senegalese are devoted followers of Sufi saints) yet devotedly fun-loving, is a magnet for musicians from across West Africa, drawn by a thriving CD market, famous venues and the best recording facilities in the region. The principal sounds are mbalax – the frenetic, drum-driven style popularized by Youssou N'Dour and his Super Etoile band – and hip-hop, whose ambassadors Daara J introduced the Senegalese streets to the world.

Going out in Dakar is not only about music and mating: clued-up Dakarois are obsessed with the mercurial fashion scene. However you wear it, your look is very important; go for bold and shiny and you won't fail to impress. Of late the girls have all been adopting singer Viviane N'Dour's cut-offs-and-skimpy-top style, a daring innovation in a country where yards of beaten damask cloth is still a byword for glamour.

need to know

Clubbing in Dakar is usually a Friday to Sunday affair. The serious business of the evening, the soirée, rarely starts before midnight, though a 7pm *matinée* is sometimes scheduled too. Hire a cab for the night and check out *Thiossane*, to see if Youssou N'Dour is in town; *Le Kily* (also called *Kilimandjaro*), home to local superstar Thione Seck; or Just 4 You, for the very grown-up Orchestra Baobab. The monthly *221* magazine has all the latest listings.

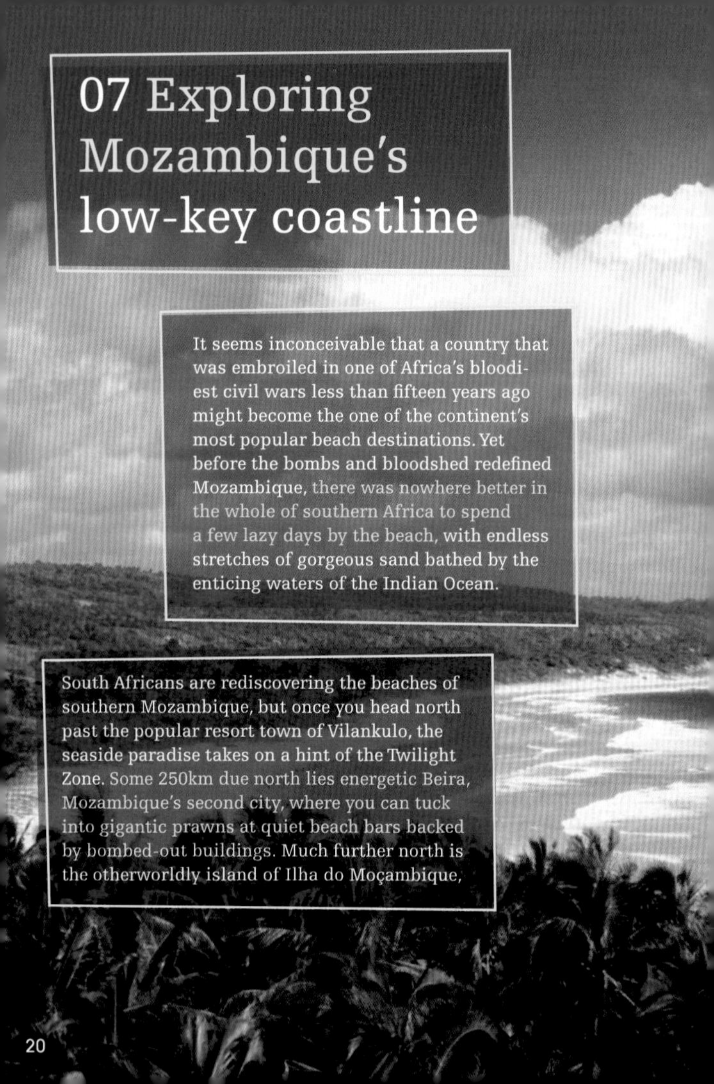

07 Exploring Mozambique's low-key coastline

It seems inconceivable that a country that was embroiled in one of Africa's bloodiest civil wars less than fifteen years ago might become the one of the continent's most popular beach destinations. Yet before the bombs and bloodshed redefined Mozambique, there was nowhere better in the whole of southern Africa to spend a few lazy days by the beach, with endless stretches of gorgeous sand bathed by the enticing waters of the Indian Ocean.

South Africans are rediscovering the beaches of southern Mozambique, but once you head north past the popular resort town of Vilankulo, the seaside paradise takes on a hint of the Twilight Zone. Some 250km due north lies energetic Beira, Mozambique's second city, where you can tuck into gigantic prawns at quiet beach bars backed by bombed-out buildings. Much further north is the otherworldly island of Ilha do Moçambique,

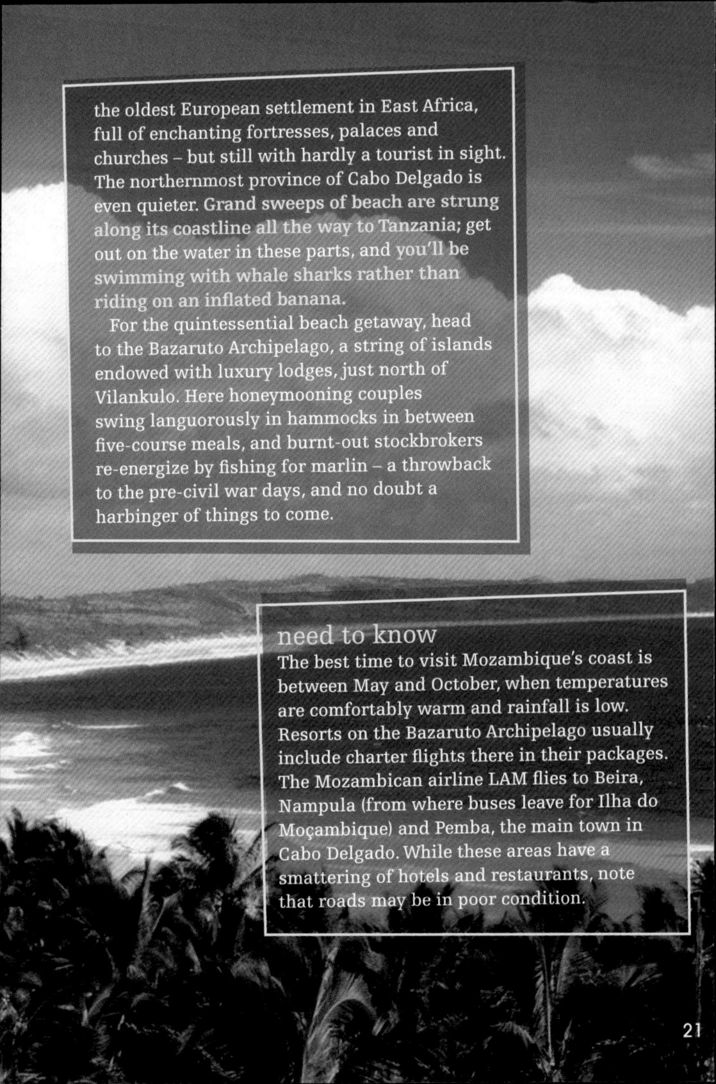

the oldest European settlement in East Africa, full of enchanting fortresses, palaces and churches – but still with hardly a tourist in sight. The northernmost province of Cabo Delgado is even quieter. Grand sweeps of beach are strung along its coastline all the way to Tanzania; get out on the water in these parts, and you'll be swimming with whale sharks rather than riding on an inflated banana.

For the quintessential beach getaway, head to the Bazaruto Archipelago, a string of islands endowed with luxury lodges, just north of Vilankulo. Here honeymooning couples swing languorously in hammocks in between five-course meals, and burnt-out stockbrokers re-energize by fishing for marlin – a throwback to the pre-civil war days, and no doubt a harbinger of things to come.

need to know

The best time to visit Mozambique's coast is between May and October, when temperatures are comfortably warm and rainfall is low. Resorts on the Bazaruto Archipelago usually include charter flights there in their packages. The Mozambican airline LAM flies to Beira, Nampula (from where buses leave for Ilha do Moçambique) and Pemba, the main town in Cabo Delgado. While these areas have a smattering of hotels and restaurants, note that roads may be in poor condition.

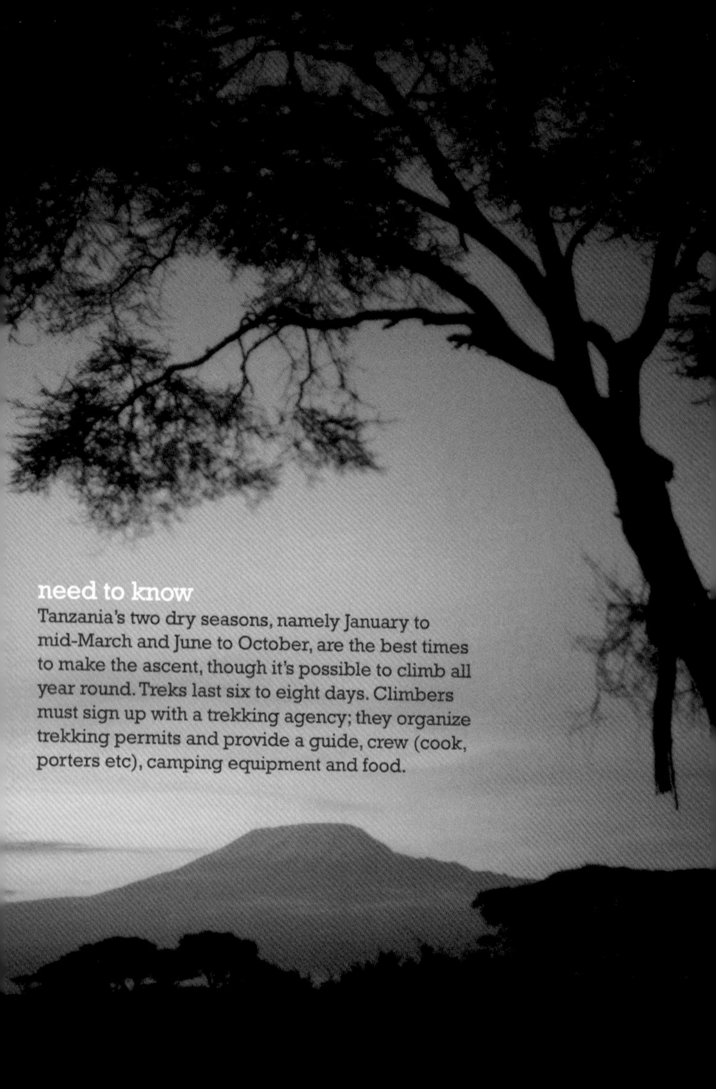

need to know

Tanzania's two dry seasons, namely January to mid-March and June to October, are the best times to make the ascent, though it's possible to climb all year round. Treks last six to eight days. Climbers must sign up with a trekking agency; they organize trekking permits and provide a guide, crew (cook, porters etc), camping equipment and food.

08 CLIMBING KILIMANJARO

The statistics are impressive. Measuring some 40km across and rising 5895m above sea level, Kilimanjaro is easily Africa's highest mountain.

But such bald facts fail to capture the thrill of actually climbing it: the days spent tramping from muggy montane forest to snowy summit, pausing occasionally to admire the views over the lush lower slopes and beyond to the dusty plains, or scrutinize the unique mountain flora; the blissful evenings gazing at the panoply of stars with fellow trekkers; and the wonderful esprit de corps that builds between yourself and your crew, a camaraderie that grows with every step until, exhausted, you stand together at the highest point in Africa.

Beguiling though the mountain may be, those contemplating an assault on Kili should consider its hazards and hardships. For one thing, though it's possible to walk to the summit of Kili, it's not easy. An iron will and calves of steel are both essential, for this is a mountain that really tests your mettle. Then there are the extreme discomforts on the slopes, from sweat-drenched shirts in the sweltering forest to frozen water bottles and wind-blasted faces at the summit. And there's the altitude itself, inducing headaches and nausea for those who ascend too fast.

Such privations, however, are totally eclipsed by the exhilaration of watching the sunrise from the Roof of Africa, with an entire continent seemingly spread out beneath you. The sense of fulfilment that courses through you on the mountaintop will stay with you, long after you've finally said goodbye to Kili.

Just being within earshot of the thundering spectacle that is Victoria Falls, a hundred-metre cataract plunging from the broad upper Zambezi into the narrow gorge below, is enough to get the adrenaline pumping. It's little wonder that the falls are such a draw for adventure-sport freaks. There's a dizzying menu of activities on offer in the nearby towns of Livingstone (on the Zambian side) and Victoria Falls (in Zimbabwe), from bungy jumping to one of the most thrilling white-water rafting runs in the world.

But the falls themselves are the star, and there's no shortage of operators offering airborne "Flight of Angels" tours. The name derives from David Livingstone's much-quoted impression of the Zambezi as he approached the falls by dugout canoe in 1855, the very first European to do so. "Scenes so lovely," he later wrote, "must have been gazed upon by angels in their flight." Today you can get an angel's-eye view by helicopter, light aircraft, microlight or even Tiger Moth.

For sheer visceral drama, microlighting is hard to beat. It's as different from the popular helicopter option as riding pillion on a motorbike is from travelling by minibus. Firmly strapped into the back seat, you can chat to the pilot through your headset. With no walls or windows to obstruct your view, you feel totally connected to the elements. Your heart will soar as you circle the mighty falls, dipping into their misty breath and losing count of the rainbows.

09 Microlighting over Victoria Falls

need to know

Mosi-oa-Tunya National Park (named after the local name for the falls, meaning "The Smoke That Thunders"), is open from 6am to 6pm; admission is $10. The falls are at their mightiest from February to May; from October to December the flow is much reduced. Microlight flights typically cost around $90 for fifteen minutes. The area has a good mix of accommodation, from budget lodges to comfortable hotels.

When Tunisia gained its independence in 1956, its then president, Habib Bourguiba, proclaimed a new nation in which "people will no longer live in caves, like animals". He was addressing the reality that across the arid far south of the country, people did live in caves, not uncommonly with their livestock. Gradually, these people were moved into new houses put up by the government, and most of the cave dwellings were abandoned.

10 Touring troglodyte villages in Tunisia

Visit the troglodyte villages today, however, and you'll find them enjoying a new lease of life – some even offer tourist accommodation. Many are stunningly sited.
At Chenini, Douiret and Guermessa, set in a jagged prehistoric landscape, you're confronted by mountainsides riddled with cave dwellings and guarded by rugged stone forts. At nearby Ghoumrassen, three folds of a rocky spur are studded with cave dwellings, under the gaze of a whitewashed mosque. Yet more scenic is Toujane, built on two sides of a gorge, with breathtaking views. Anywhere you might spot oil stains down the hillside, signifying caves housing ancient olive presses; visit after the olive harvest and you'll may well see some of these being powered by donkeys.

But the big centre for troglodyte homes is Matmata, whose people live, to this day, in pit dwellings. Signs outside some invite you to visit, and for a few dinars you can descend into a central courtyard dug deep into soft sandstone, which serves to keep the rooms – excavated into the sides – comfortably cool in summer and warm in winter. Better still, Matmata has three hotels in converted pit dwellings, including the *Sidi Driss*, which was used as one of the locations in *Star Wars* – here you can dine where Luke Skywalker once did.

need to know

Spring and autumn are the best times to visit southern Tunisia. Public transport to Matmata is fairly regular, but services to the other villages are sporadic. Troglodyte accommodation, all reasonably priced, ranges from Matmata's deluxe *Hôtel Diar el Barbar*, where the caves are decked out with all mod cons, to simple guesthouses in Douiret and Toujane.

11 SAMPLING WINES IN THE WESTERN CAPE

We're sitting around the elegant dining table of a 200-year-old Cape Dutch manor house, set in beautiful countryside near Paarl. Our host, effusive wine expert Katinka van Niekerk, has us under strict instructions to sample the heavenly wines before us in a pre-planned order. Before each mouthful, we must eat something of a particular flavour or texture – curry for spice, cheese for sweetness, bread to neutralize the palate once again – and note the effects. It's fascinating stuff.

When we're asked to wash down a piece of bread and Marmite with a mouthful of vintage Pinotage, master winemaker Razvan Macici, who has joined us for this session, grimaces. The Marmite represents the flavour known as **umami**, also found in soy sauce, Parmesan and certain mushrooms. It wrecks Pinotage, the signature Cape red. But the same wine with a chunk of roast lamb tastes like a dream.

Earlier in the day we toured the massive Nederburg estate, admiring the ranks of vines which stretch away to the purple-tinged Drakenstein Mountains, sniffing the heady, oaky aromas of the barrel rooms and marvelling at the cellars' hi-tech temperature-controlled steel tanks. Then it was time for our first tasting. We all eyed the spitoons rather squeamishly and went for what seemed, at the time, the more decorous option – raising each glass to our noses to inhale the bouquet and then taking delicate sips.

It's amazing how quickly all those sips add up. So it is that when, replete from our wine-and-food-pairing lunch, we stagger out onto the lawn to enjoy the sunshine and spring flowers, we're all merrily speaking double Dutch.

NEED TO KNOW

Many wineries around Stellenbosch, Franschhoek and Paarl – all within 70km of Cape Town – open their cellars to the public from November to March, some year-round. A variety of wine-route tours, suitable for everyone from specialist connoisseurs to casual tipplers, can be booked in Stellenbosch. It's easy enough to plan your own self-drive tour – as long as the designated driver is happy to stay sober.

The mountain gorilla sequence from *Life on Earth* made television history, and inspired a generation of armchair nature-lovers to set off into some of Africa's darkest, sweatiest crevices.

12 Tracking mountain gorillas in Uganda

While David Attenborough's encounter took place in Rwanda's Virunga Mountains, the nearby Bwindi Impenetrable National Park, where roughly half the world's mountain gorillas live, is a popular alternative. Getting to Bwindi, in Uganda's far southeast, is challenging, admission is pricey and trekking through the dense, hilly rainforest strictly for the fit and determined (they don't call this the Impenetrable Forest for nothing). But having at last caught your first glimpse of a dark eye and a salt-and-pepper back, you'll be replaying the moment in your mind for the rest of your life.

You're no longer allowed to get quite as close to the mighty beasts as Attenborough, who tumbled around in the wild celery, grinning at the cameras while making restrained burping noises to put the gorillas at their ease. These days, the rules are to keep a good few metres away and avoid prolonged eye contact. You should also resist the urge to leg it if threatened or (heaven forbid) charged. Silverbacks, the big males, are all front, apparently; if, when challenged, you crouch submissively in the undergrowth, they'll be satisfied you know your place.

It's wise, too, to keep your photographic ambitions modest; the lighting can be dim and your subjects may be shy. Instead, relax and focus on the little details – gestures, interactions and looks – and you'll enjoy a magical hour in the gorillas' company.

need to know

The best times to track gorillas are June to September and December to January, when conditions are relatively dry. A permit costs $375 including park and guide fees, bookable in advance from the Uganda Wildlife Authority office (Ⓦwww.uwa.or.ug). Simple accommodation is available at the community-run rest camp near the park headquarters at Buhoma, ten hours' drive from Kampala.

13

Hiking through Mali's Dogon Country

Despite their isolation in a hot, harsh tract of central Mali, the Dogon people have been visited over the centuries by tribal warlords and French colonialists. Happily, the Dogon have managed to preserve many of their traditional ways, including living close to a dramatic, rusty-ochre sandstone cliff, the Bandiagara Escarpment, in tightly clustered mudbrick houses with shaggy-roofed granaries.

Today, most visitors to Dogon Country are hardy travellers. Some walk from village to village along ancient trails, but you can also travel by donkey cart or motorbike. Along the way, you can admire mud mosques with organic, curvy crenellations, and catch your breath in the shade of baobabs which look older than time. In the villages themselves, you'll find walls, doors and ceremonial masks decorated with symbols derived from the Dogons' intricate belief system, and you can visit sacred altars marked by odd porridge-smeared fetishes. At some point, you're likely to be offered a half-calabash of millet beer, perhaps containing the odd bug doing the backstroke – never has homebrew tasted so refreshing.

Africa still has plenty of remote corners where light pollution is unknown, and the night sky is a dazzling dome of stars. There's nowhere better to enjoy the show than in Dogon Country, a region whose inhabitants' knowledge of the cosmos has fascinated anthropologists for decades. At nightfall, climb a notched-plank ladder to spread your mattress on the flat roof of a village house, then lie back to enjoy that fabulous, 360-degree celestial view.

need to know

The most popular entry point to the Dogon region is the village of Bandiagara, 12km from the edge of the escarpment. Transport there, and guides, can be arranged in the nearby town of Mopti. Each Dogon village will levy small charges for visiting and for basic food (such as couscous or rice with peanut sauce) and accommodation. The best weather for walking is November to January; March to May is extremely hot. June to September, the rainy season, is humid, but the air is clear and there's the added bonus of waterfalls, flowers and foliage.

14 Soaking in Wikki Warm Springs

Bathing in the near-perfect natural pool at Wikki Warm Springs, part of Nigeria's remote Yankari National Park, is simply one of West Africa's most gratifying experiences. Below the park lodge, down a steep path, the upper Gaji stream bubbles up from a deep cleft beneath a rose-coloured, sandstone cliff. Twelve million litres a day, at a constant 31°C, flood out over sparkling sand between a dense bank of overhanging tropical foliage on one side, and the concrete apron that serves as a beach on the other – the one dud note in an otherwise picture-perfect environment, though the concrete helps keep the crystal-clear water clean. Floodlighting makes the springs equally idyllic at night, giving them a satisfyingly theatrical appearance, like an elaborate bit of New Age interior design.

A good deal larger than most swimming pools, the springs are the ideal place to wash away the frustrations of travel in Nigeria. But should you tire of simply drifting on your back above the gentle current, you can explore the woods around the lodge for their abundant birdlife. It's also possible to go with Yankari's rangers on a guided game drive in a battered old truck, bringing you into close contact with the park's large elephant population, and opportunities to see a wide variety of antelope and other savanna mammals. If, as occasionally happens, the viewing isn't up to much, returning to Wikki Warm Springs, and that delightful initial immersion, is more than ample compensation.

need to know

Yankari is popular with vacationing expats and better-off Nigerian families, and can get crowded at weekends, especially over Christmas and Easter. The park lodge has very basic rooms, which should be reserved ahead at the park office in Bauchi, 117km to the northeast (Ⓣ077/543 674). Simple meals and a bar are also available. Watch out for your belongings as you swim: the park's baboons are expert thieves and missile dodgers.

15 The Festival in the Desert

Right back to pre-Islamic times, Tuareg nomads would have gathered in the desert to settle disputes, race camels and entertain one another with displays of swordsmanship, music and dance. Today, Mali's Festival in the Desert combines these traditions with the chance to hear a dazzling range of African sounds under the clear desert sky. The music and the setting among the rolling white dunes of the southern Sahara are hard to beat, but it's the people – men in richly coloured robes perched on camels bedecked with tassles; women in black, their faces stained with indigo – and the sea of white tents where families have set up camp with their livestock that make the event so unforgettable.

By day most of the action takes place in and around a shallow natural amphitheatre where women drum, clap and sing and tribesmen dance, swiping swords through the air as they skip and sway to the hypnotic rhythms. Stalls nearby sell metal and leatherwork, beads of glass and amber and moon-faced fertility dolls. Here you can have a cloth-seller

tie you a turban against the burning sun, or learn about nomadic life as you bargain over glasses of bittersweet Tuareg tea.

After nightfall, as temperatures plummet, you'll be wrapping up warm and planting yourself close to one of the charcoal braziers among the dunes. From the one proper stage, the festival's main acts pump out an astonishing range of music, from the pure, limpid tones of the harp-like kora to timeless desert blues of the kind made famous by the late, great Ali Farka Toure.

need to know

The festival takes place over a long weekend in early January at Essakane, several hours of off-road driving northwest from Timbuktu (a 4WD is required; Timbuktu itself has flights from the capital, Bamako). Festival tickets, including basic accommodation in shared tents and three simple meals a day (meat stew and rice, soup and rock-hard Tuareg bread baked in the sand) can be purchased in advance from Ⓦwww.festival-au-desert.org for $400. Some specialist agents include the festival as part of a Mali package itinerary.

16 STROLLING THROUGH THE RUINS OF LEPTIS MAGNA

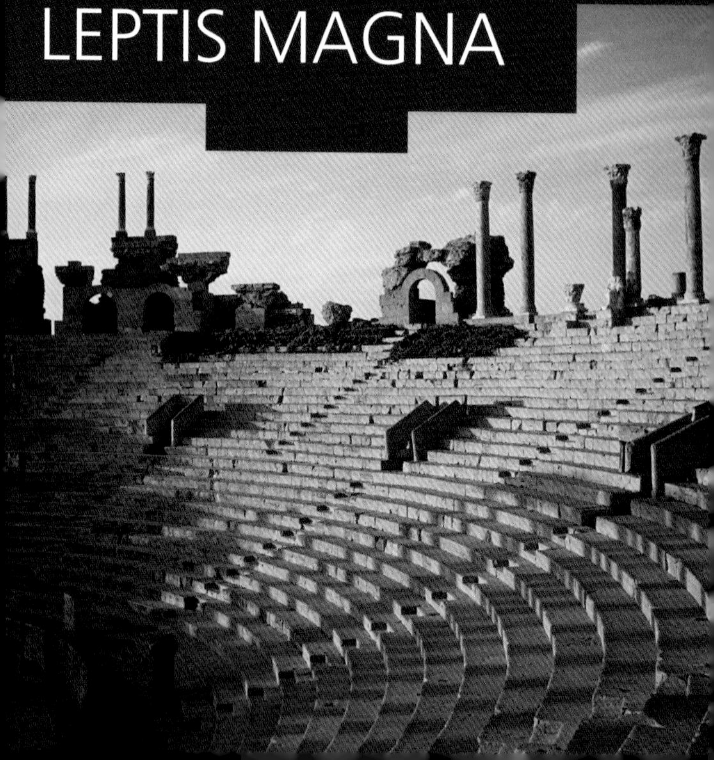

North Africa is dotted with Roman remains, but the one that beats them all is Leptis Magna, arguably the most impressive Roman site outside Pompeii.

Leptis Magna reached its zenith under local boy Septimius Severus, who rose to become emperor in 193 AD, and died in battle eighteen years later in a far-flung province called Britain. Fittingly, if there's one superlative edifice at Leptis Magna, it's the amazing four-way arch Septimius commissioned. One of the first monuments you encounter, it's nearly forty metres tall, and bears a plethora of superb marble reliefs, recently restored. Septimius also endowed the city with the more impressive of its two forums, squares where people met to socialize and conduct business. Strewn though it now is with fallen columns, you can stand in the middle of it and still feel awed by its size and grandeur.

So well preserved is the city's luxurious bathhouse, endowed by Septimius's predecessor, Hadrian, that it's easily recognizable as a direct ancestor of the hammams found across North Africa. Walking through, you follow the route that bathers took, from the frigidarium (cold room) through the tepidarium (warm room, but actually more like an open-air swimming pool) to the caldarium (hot room), where they would sweat out the grime and scrub it off – just as in a today's hammams.

Elsewhere, there's an enormous amphitheatre (for gladiatorial and other sporting events, possibly involving Christians and lions), a hippodrome (for horse races) and a substantial, well-preserved theatre to take in, among other remains. There's also a good museum with commentaries in English. But one of the very best things to do at Leptis Magna is simply to wander the maze of colonnaded streets, so intact that you can imagine toga-clad Romans approaching at every corner.

need to know

Leptis Magna is just 3km east of the Libyan town of Khoms, which has a sprinkling of accommodation, though it's easy enough to make a day-trip from Tripoli, just an hour's drive to the west. Spring and autumn are the best times to visit.

17 On foot in the Kruger

The word "safari" comes from the Swahili for "walk", though these days most wildlife-spotters prefer to take a 4x4; in the vast Kruger National Park, South Africa's best-known wildlife destination, the standard way to view game is from the network of tarred roads which crisscross the savanna.

Yet there is nothing to compare to a stroll in the bush for getting close to nature. All your senses are engaged. You smell the bush, and you hear it; snapping twigs begin to sound as loud – and sometimes as ominous – as they do in the movies. There's the adrenaline rush of playing peek-a-boo with a rhino or a giraffe, while at the same time the whole game-viewing experience becomes much more than a tick list of the big animals: you realize that butterflies and flowers, trees and dung beetles are just as interesting, and you'll find yourself fascinated by "spoor" – footprints, tracks or droppings. You won't see fences or cars or other people, but you might see something that can eat you. It might see you. Hey, that's nature.

need to know

There are seven wilderness trails in Kruger National Park, mostly in the southern section, around 450km east of Johannesburg. Trails cost around $400 per person and involve three nights' sleeping and eating in rustic style out in the bush, with long dawn walks and shorter late-afternoon forays from base camp in the company of armed rangers. Heavily subscribed, the trails have to be booked up to a year in advance through South African National Parks (Ⓦwww.sanparks.org).

18 Sun, sea and slave forts: Ghana's coast

In 1471, Portuguese merchant seamen arrived on the palm-lined shore of the Gold Coast and built a fort at Elmina.

They were followed over the next 400 years by the British, Dutch, Swedes, Danes, and Baltic adventurers. Gold was their first desire, but the slave trade soon became the coast's dominant activity, and more than three dozen forts were established here, largely to run the exchange of human cargo for cloth, liquor and guns. Today, thirty forts still stand, several in dramatic locations and offering atmospheric tours and accommodation. Here you can combine poignant historical discovery with time on the beach – a rare blend in this part of the world.

One of the biggest forts is the seventeenth-century Cape Coast castle, which dominates the teeming town of the same name. Just walking through its claustrophobic dungeons, where slaves were once held before being shipped across the Atlantic, can be harrowing for some visitors. A particularly good time to visit the town is in September, when the huge harvest festival, the Oguaa Fetu, takes over in a noisy, palm-wine-lubricated parade of chiefs, fetish priests and queen mothers. If you want to be made particularly welcome, bring along some schnapps, the customary gift for traditional rulers, with whom you may well be granted an audience.

Elmina, now a bustling fishing port, is home to the photogenically sited St George's Castle and Fort St Jago, eyeballing each other across the lagoon. St George's offers a worthwhile historical and cultural exhibition, and in the town itself you can ogle several intricate traditional shrines – pastel-coloured edifices of platforms, arches and militaristic figurines.

Some of the best beaches are at Busua, which has a low-key resort an easy walk from the cutely perched Fort Metal Cross. A day-trip to the far western coast, between Princestown and Axim, brings you to an even finer stretch of beaches and sandy coves, punctuated by jungle-swathed headlands.

need to know

Bus services run along the main coastal highway from Accra. For the simple comforts of fort accommodation, expect to pay $5–10 per person per night.

The tectonic forces that created East Africa's Great Rift Valley also threw up a rash of volcanoes, one of which blew itself to smithereens 2.5 million years ago. Its legacy, the nineteen-kilometre-wide Ngorongoro Crater, is a place that holiday brochures like to call "the eighth wonder of the world". They're not far wrong. Ngorongoro's natural amphitheatre is home to virtually every emblematic animal species you might want to see in Africa, and the crater's deep, bluish-purple sides provide spectacular backdrops to any photograph.

The magic begins long before you reach the crater. As you ascend from the Rift Valley along a series of hairpins, the extent of the region's geological tumult becomes breathtakingly apparent. Continuing up through **liana-draped forest**, you're suddenly at the crater's edge, surveying an ever-changing patchwork of green and yellow hues **streaked with shadows and mist**.

Living in the crater's grasslands, swamps, glades and lakes is Africa's highest density of predators – **lions** and **leopards**, **hyenas** and **jackals**

19 Wildlife-spotting in

among them – for whom a sumptuous banquet of antelope and other delicacies awaits. **Glimpsing lions is an unforgettable thrill;** just as memorable but far more unsettling is the macabre excitement of witnessing a kill. You'll also see **elephants** and **black rhino**, the latter poached to the brink of extinction. Twitchers have plenty to go for, too, including **swashes of pink flamingoes** adorning the alkaline Lake Magadi in the Crater's heart. If ogling wildlife from a vehicle doesn't do it for you, stretch your legs – and escape the crowds – on a hike through the Crater Highlands, in the company of an armed ranger and a Maasai guide.

need to know

Crater safaris are easily arranged in Arusha, several hours' drive to the east, starting at $120 a day. The mid-range and upmarket lodges on the crater rim have great views but are far from intimate. Preferable are the "special campsites", all well located, quieter and cheaper, but these need to be booked months in advance.

the Ngorongoro Crater

20 Discovering Rock Art On The Tassili N'Ajjer Plateau

The world's biggest open-air art gallery lurks in the heart of the Sahara, among the wind-carved ramparts of southeastern Algeria's Tassili N'Ajjer plateau.

Its caves and overhangs shelter countless prehistoric images, customarily termed frescoes, **laboriously engraved or painted onto the rock in shades of ochre,** white and charcoal black. When discovered in the 1930s, these images – including elephants, hippos and rhinos – helped illustrate the dramatic influence climate change has had on human development.

The most impressive concentration of rock-art sites is on the **plateau above the remote oasis of Djanet.** When, after an hour's steep hike, you finally encounter the frescoes for the first time, it's a humbling experience, heightened by the arid desolation. **Was the Sahara once so green that right where you stand, women would grind corn or milk cows alongside flowing rivers, as some frescoes depict?**

These scenes, some as fine as on any Greek vase, reflect the main theme of the frescoes, that of the Neolithic Revolution, when humans turned from eons of hunter-gathering to a settled lifestyle tending crops and domesticating animals. Not all such attempts were ultimately successful though – **look out for engravings of giraffes on leads.**

Elsewhere, figures with large round heads don't depict spacemen, as once theorized, but arcane gods, presaging the dawn of religious consciousness. Subsequently, the descendants of the ancient hunters are shown turning their bows and spears on each other as horse-drawn charioteers invade from the north. **The story ends as the current arid phase takes hold, driving the people of the Tassili towards the Mediterranean and the Nile valley. The rest, as they say, is history.**

need to know

Between October and March, there are weekly flights from Paris to Djanet, costing around $660. **Most Tassili treks are part of a fortnight's organized tour in the Djanet region** (around $2000). Written confirmation of your place on a tour is required to obtain an Algerian visa. **A useful source of tour-agency contacts is ⓦwww.sahara-overland.com.**

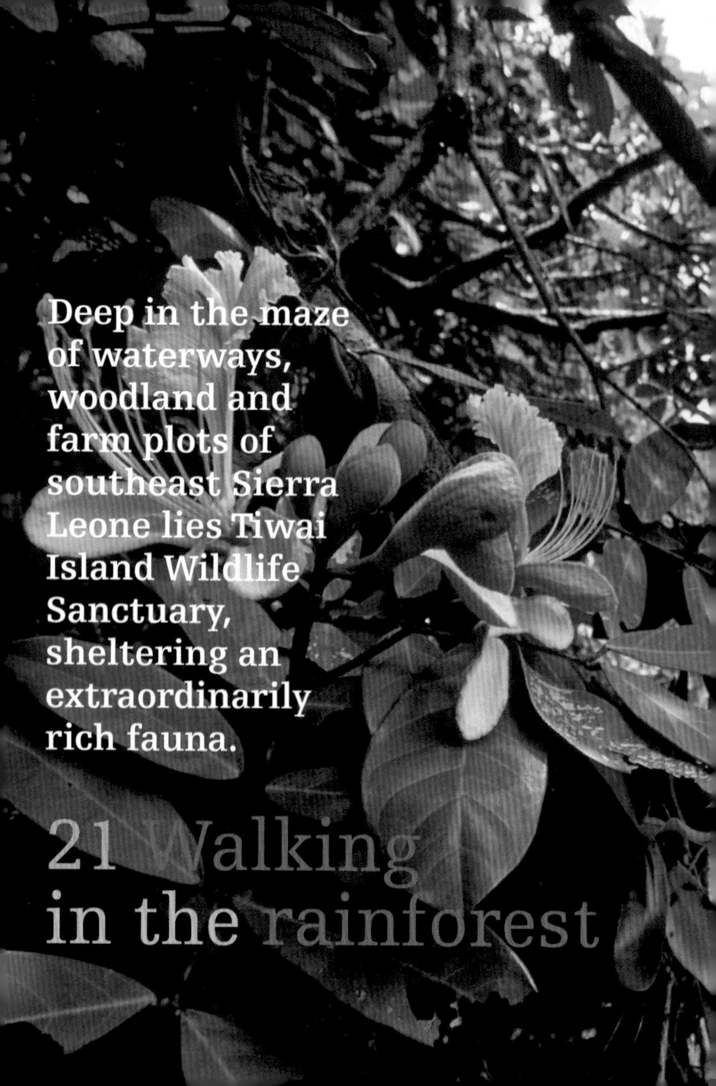

Deep in the maze of waterways, woodland and farm plots of southeast Sierra Leone lies Tiwai Island Wildlife Sanctuary, sheltering an extraordinarily rich fauna.

21 Walking in the rainforest

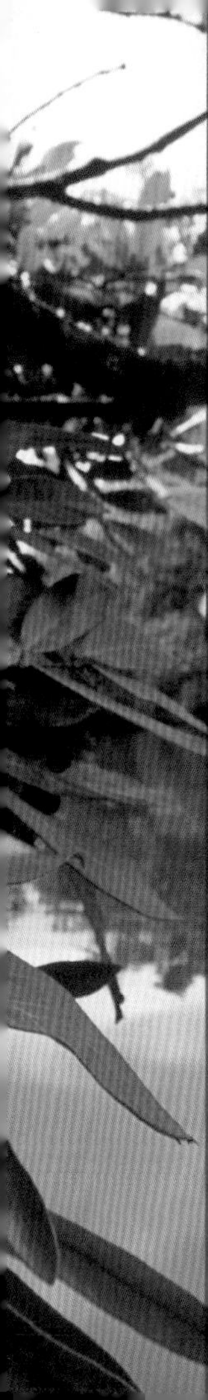

This truly is the Africa of the imagination, the air saturated with the incessant chirrups, squawks and yelps of birds, chimpanzees and monkeys, tree hyraxes, assorted insects and hundreds of other creatures, all doing their thing in twelve square kilometres of rainforest. In the background, you can hear the dim rush of the Moa River where it splits to roar around Tiwai through rocks and channels.

As you weave along paths between the giant buttress roots of the trees, park guides will track troops of colobus and diana monkeys and should know where the chimps are. The rarest and most secretive of Tiwai's denizens is the hog-sized pygmy hippo, which you're not likely to see unless you go jungle walking at night, when they traipse their habitual solitary paths through the undergrowth.

Exploring after dark with a guide is, in fact, highly recommended – take a lamp with plenty of kerosene, and a good torch. By night, the forest is a powerful presence, with an immense, consuming vigour: every rotten branch teems with termites. All around, you sense the organs of detection of a million unseen creatures waving at your illuminated figure as you stumble over the roots. Of course, if you prefer not to get lost, take a GPS unit.

need to know

With the return of peace and order, Sierra Leone once again is safe to visit; a useful source of general tourist information is Ⓦwww.visitsierraleone.org. Take public transport to Potoru and motorbike taxi from there to the riverbank at Kambama, from where you can glide across to Tiwai in a low, slim dugout. The visitors' centre offers a communal lounge, showers and toilets, tents under roofs and a kitchen area.

22 *Exploring* Namibia's Skeleton Coast

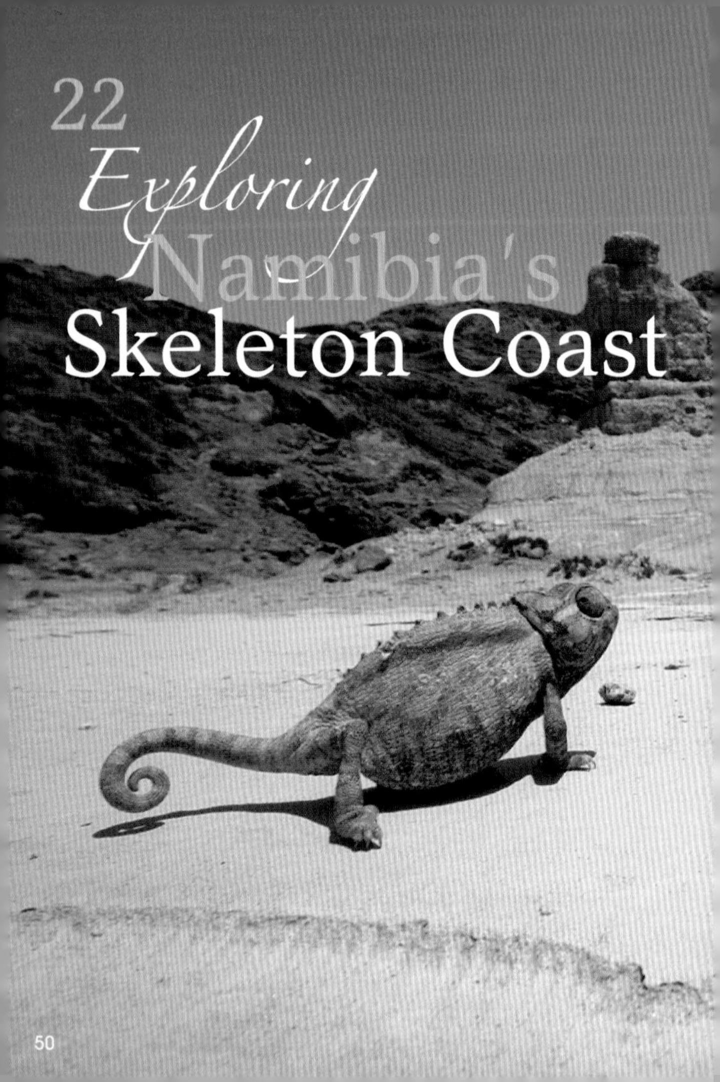

Namibia's extreme northwest is called the Skeleton Coast, with good reason. Its treacherous conditions have scuppered ships – the beach is littered with rusting iron and weathered timbers from long-abandoned wrecks – and whales, too, have met their end here, their massive vertebrae bleaching on the shore, lapped by the tides

As a visitor, you'll need an eye for detail to appreciate the allure of this bleak and barren place, **where the chilly Atlantic meets mountainous dunes and endless, grey-white gravel plains**, and distant wind-sculpted rocks cast unearthly shadows. Look carefully and you'll begin to realize that **the desert is not as devoid of life as it might seem**. Walking through the rugged landscapes with a guide, you'll learn how beetles, lizards and sidewinder adders survive on the moisture brought by the early morning mists. You may begin to distinguish the different lichens – delicate smudges of black, white and ginger which decorate slabs of quartz and basalt. **Drought-resistant succulents like the bizarre, pebble-like lithops** and the ragged, ancient-looking *Welwitschia mirabilis* cling to life in the gravel. Among the few mammals hardy enough to survive in this environment are **black-backed jackals and noisy, malodorous colonies of Cape fur seals**, the latter a potential target for hungry lions, which very occasionally can be seen prowling the shoreline.

Perhaps the **best way to enjoy the desert's strange beauty is from the air.** Soar over the landscape in a light aircraft and you f**eel like an astronaut over an alien world**, the scene below mottled and textured like a vast abstract painting.

need to know

Most visitors book a package, including guided nature walks and 4x4 excursions, at the only formal accommodation, ***Skeleton Coast Camp*** (Ⓦwww.wilderness-safaris.com), a luxury tented camp reachable only by air. Scenic flights over the region can be arranged in Swakopmund, 200km to the south. High season is July to October.

23 Island-hopping in Cape Verde

Follow the pointing finger of Senegal westwards and, 400km off the African coast, you reach the archipelago of Cape Verde, home of soulful world-music superstar Cesaria Evora. This nation of nine small islands was uninhabited until colonized by the Portuguese in 1462. The new arrivals brought in slaves from the mainland to work their sugar-cane fields. Not quite Africa and not quite European, Cape Verde today is almost Brazilian in feel.

Start in Praia, the capital, dramatically sited on a plateau on the largest and greenest island, Santiago, and offering relaxed street life, a small museum and a scattering of restaurants and clubs. From here, take the thirty-minute flight to Fogo ("Fire") island, dominated by a vast volcanic crater, where Cape Verde's only vineyards flourish. It's surmounted by the cone of a more recent volcano, steep but climbable, with sweeping views across the Atlantic from the summit that fully justify the effort.

The flat, desert islands of the east – Sal, Maio, Boa Vista – have all the best beaches, azure seas and windsurfing schools. On Boa Vista you can rent a jeep and drive to the uninhabited south coast, where turtle tracks are almost the only sign of life, and Robinson Crusoe images spring irresistibly to mind.

Out on the northwest fringe of the archipelago lies the canyon-grooved mass of Santo Antão, where local buses cut precipitous routes along nineteenth-century cobbled roads overlooking the ocean. It's one of the more fertile islands, and you can enjoy superb hikes along rural farmers' paths. Nearby is São Vicente, most noteworthy for playing host to an exuberant Carnaval every February, and the international Baia das Gatas music festival every August.

So what would you eat and drink in Cape Verde? Typical is pork or tuna, in a hybrid of Portuguese and African styles, washed down with shots of grogue, a powerful, aromatic sugar-cane rum.

need to know

There are regular flights to Cape Verde from Manchester, Lisbon, Paris and Boston. You can get around the islands by ferry, but voyages can be rough and slow; alternatively, buy a multi-coupon domestic air ticket on TACV, the national airline.

24 HANGING OUT IN THE JEMAA EL FNA, MARRAKESH

There's nowhere on earth like the Jemaa el Fna, the square at the heart of old Marrakesh. The focus of the evening promenade for Marrakshis, the Jemaa is a heady blend of alfresco food bazaar and street theatre: for as long as you're in town, you'll want to come back here again and again.

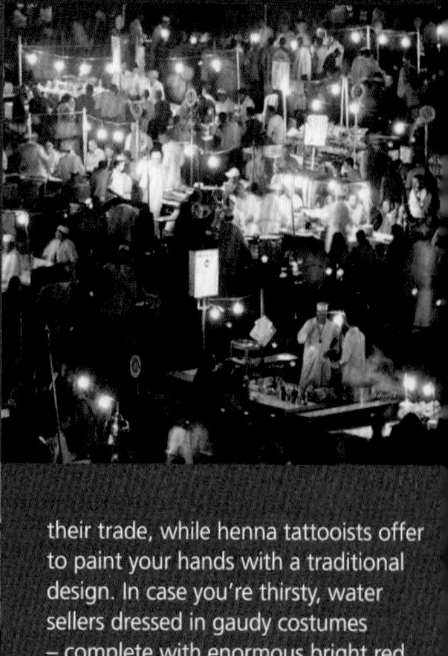

Goings-on in the square by day merely hint at the evening's spectacle. Breeze through and you'll stumble upon a few snake charmers, toothpullers and medicine men plying their trade, while henna tattooists offer to paint your hands with a traditional design. In case you're thirsty, water sellers dressed in gaudy costumes – complete with enormous bright red hats – vie for your custom alongside a line of stalls offering orange and grapefruit juice, pressed on the spot.

Around dusk however, you'll find yourself swept up in a pulsating circus of performers. There are acrobats from the Atlas mountains, dancers in drag, and musicians from a religious brotherhood called the Gnaoua, chanting and beating out rhythms late into the night with their clanging iron castanets. Other groups play Moroccan folk music, while storytellers, heirs to an ancient tradition, draw raucous crowds to hear their tales.

In their midst dozens of food stalls set up, lit by gas lanterns and surrounded

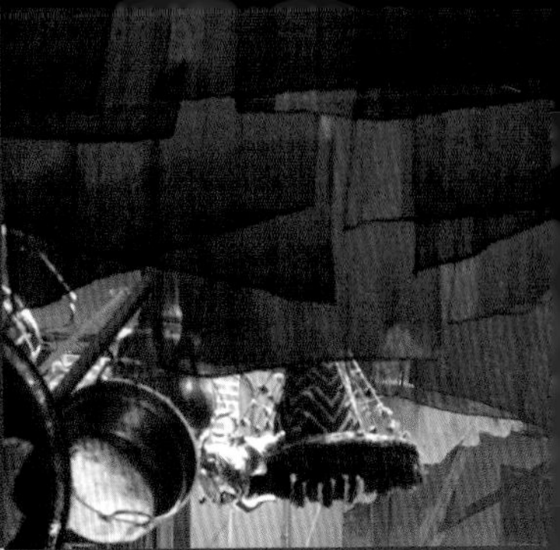

need to know

Marrakesh has reasonable air links with Europe, including flights operated by a couple of budget airlines. Given that summers are very hot and winters surprisingly chilly, the city is best visited in spring or autumn. There's a massive choice of accommodation around the Jemaa, notably some lovely riads – old houses set around patio gardens, done out as boutique hotels.

by delicious-smelling plumes of cooking smoke. Here you can partake of spicy *harira* soup, try charcoal-roasted kebabs or *merguez* sausage, or, if you're really adventurous, a whole sheep's head, including the eyes – all beneath the looming presence of the floodlit, perfectly proportioned Koutoubia minaret to the west, making a backdrop without compare.

25 Wandering LAMU ISLAND

At the northern end of the Kenyan coast lies the magical Lamu archipelago. Fringed by sandy beaches and mangrove forests, this clutch of islands is the northern centre of Swahili civilization, the blend of African and Persian Gulf cultures that formed a thousand years ago as traders from the Middle East settled among Bantu-speaking farmers and fishers.

Visit the town of Lamu, on the island of the same name, and you'll discover an endlessly diverting warren of alleys and multi-storeyed stone houses, some dating back hundreds of years, all built around an interior courtyard. Devoid of cars, and full of quiet corners and arresting street scenes – donkeys bearing TVs, a turbaned man with a swordfish – the town is best appreciated by serendipity, and there is plenty to chance upon, including two dozen old mosques and various colonial-style waterfront buildings. And as you explore, you'll encounter women in black cover-all *buibuis*, and swarthy sailors wearing the sarong known as a *kikoi*; you might even meet one of the area's traditional transvestite community. Once you've exhausted the town's nooks and crannies, at low tide you can simply walk south along the waterfront to reach the charming village of Shela, and Lamu's enticing ten-kilometre-long beach.

The most enthralling time to visit Lamu is during Maulidi (starting on March 20 in 2008), the week-long celebration of Muhammad's birth, when the entire town is swept up in processions and dances, cafés and restaurants are buzzing and locals are likely to invite you to dine with them.

need to know

Lamu is served by domestic flights and by buses from Malindi and Mombasa. There are dozens of places to stay in town, from basic lodgings at $10 a bed to luxury houses which can be rented for $400 a night. Dhow trips from the harbour are a popular diversion, costing around $20 per day per person.

Ultimate experiences Africa miscellany

1 Bush taxis

All over Africa, **bush taxis** are the classic mode of public transport. Not to be confused with the Western notion of a taxi, these vehicles travel between towns on standard routes and at fixed fares. A bush taxi can be anything from an estate car, sometimes with an extra row of seats built into the back, to a pick-up truck with benches, or even a minibus. Comfort is secondary to profit, and fare-paying passengers - and sometimes their chickens and goats - are *crammed* into every available space on board.

2 Trading places

One of the main factors that shaped the history of West Africa between the eleventh and seventeenth centuries was trans-Saharan trade. **Gold** from Buré (in modern-day Guinea), Bambouk (in modern-day Senegal) and Akan (in modern-day Ghana) was transported across the desert to North Africa, as were **slaves**, while **salt** from mines in the Sahara went south. Mighty desert trading outposts were created, such as Oualata and Aoudaghost (both in modern-day Mauritania), and most famously Timbuktu (in modern-day Mali), once so wealthy that its streets were said to be lined with gold. Huge camel caravans known as **azalaïs** still transport salt mined in Taoudenni, northern Mali, across the Sahara, though trucks and lorries are increasingly supplanting these ships of the desert.

3 Tallness, in short

Africa is home to a great variety of ethnic groups, including some of the shortest and tallest people in the world. **Pygmies**, found all over central Africa, measure on average 137cm (four and a half feet). In contrast, the average height of the **Tutsi** (or Watussi) of Rwanda and Burundi is just over 183cm (six feet).

4 Out of Africa

It's widely believed that humankind is descended from Africans. Genetic analysis indicates that humans share a common matrilineal ancestor, nicknamed **African Eve**, who lived in what is now Ethiopia, Kenya or Tanzania about 150,000 years ago, while **Adam**, the patrilineal ancestor, lived in the same general area between 60,000 and 90,000 years ago. Indigenous Africans are Eve's direct descendants, while peoples from other parts of the world are descended from African lines.

The five oldest hominid fossils discoveries

SPECIES	LOCATION DISCOVERED	DATE DISCOVERED	ESTIMATED AGE
Sahelanthropus tchadensis	Southern Sahara, Chad	2001	6–7 million years
Ardipithecus ramidus	Aramis, Ethiopia	1992–93	4.4 million years
Australopithecus anamensis	Kanapoi, Kenya	1965	4 million years
Australopithecus afarensis	Laetoli, Tanzania	1978	3.7 million years
Australopithecus afarensis	Hadar, Ethiopia	1974	3.2 million years

5 Health

Traditional medicine is widely used all over Africa, often in preference to Western forms of treatment, and can comprise anything from prayers and incantations to administering remedies derived from almost any plant or animal you can think of. Much to the dismay of sexual health campaigners, at the 2006 International AIDS Conference in Toronto, South Africa's health minister recommended a mixture of garlic, beetroot, lemon and African potatoes as an alternative to anti-retroviral drugs in the fight against **HIV**.

6 Literature

African winners of the Nobel Prize for Literature

YEAR	AUTHOR	A RECOMMENDED WORK
2003	J.M. Coetzee (South Africa)	**Life and Times of Michael K** (1983). In which the Kafka-esque character of Michael K makes a harrowing journey through an imaginary war-torn South Africa.
1991	Nadine Gordimer (South Africa)	**The Conservationist** (1974). An analysis of apartheid in South Africa, through the eyes of a wealthy white industrialist.
1986	Wole Soyinka (Nigeria)	**King Baabu** (2001). A play parodying African dictators, past and present.

"When an old man dies, it is as if a library burns down."

Amadou Hampaté Bâ (Malian writer)

7 Running

Although **athletes** from North Africa are rapidly gaining ground, it is still the **East Africans** that dominate middle- and long-distance running. Academics have long tried to explain the endurance of athletes from countries like Ethiopia and Kenya. Some researchers believe that living and training at high altitudes produces great athletes. For others, it's all a matter of genetics: for example, in the late 1980s the Nandi people comprised under two percent of Kenya's population, but made up two-fifths of the nation's elite runners.

8 Etiquette

Some rules of etiquette apply practically throughout Africa: the use of **formal greetings and handshakes** before starting a conversation; the use of the right hand to bring food to your mouth (the left hand is considered unclean, as it's used to clean yourself when going to the toilet); asking **permission** before you take someone's photograph. Of course, tribes and peoples each have their own protocols. For example, when **taking tea with the Tuareg**, who live in the Sahara and Sahel regions of North and West Africa, you will be served sickly sweet tea from a pot that is usually filled no more than three times. The first cup is said to be *fort comme la mort* (strong as death); the second *doux comme la vie* (mild as life); and the third *sucré comme l'amour* (sweet as love). If you are served a fourth cup from the same pot, you have overstayed your welcome and should leave.

"Wisdom is like a baobab tree; no one individual can embrace it."

West African saying

9 Debt

African countries owe more than **$200 billion**, mainly to rich nations and international financial institutions. They pay some **$14 billion** annually to service these debts – a trifling amount compared to, say, US defence expenditure, but for some countries, debt **repayments** can constitute as much as a third of government revenue. The importance of debt relief and fair access to global markets for African nations were highlighted by 2005's Live 8 concerts, and have become the focus of anti-poverty campaigns in many countries.

10 Kings

The powers of the kings of Morocco and Lesotho are limited by their country's constitutions, but no such check seems to be placed on Africa's last absolute monarch, **King Mswati III of Swaziland**, who has ruled in an authoritarian - and eccentric - style since 1986. In 2001 he signed a decree banning newspapers, stating afterwards: "I must admit that when I signed this decree, I did not read it at all. I just signed it." Another decree banned women under 18 having sex in an attempt to combat the country's massive HIV/AIDS problem (around forty percent of Swaziland's population is HIV positive), but just two months after imposing the ban the king himself broke it in marrying his ninth wife, who was just 16 – for which he fined himself a cow.

"We have corruption in the developed countries too but here it doesn't kill people - in Africa it does."

Bob Geldof

11 Stargazing

When, in the late 1930s, the reclusive **Dogon people** of Mali gave French anthropologist Marcel Griaule an insight into their customs and beliefs, it was apparent that they had a considerable knowledge of the heavens. They knew about Saturn's rings and four of Jupiter's moons, and claimed that Sirius, the brightest star as seen from Earth, was orbited by two other stars, one of which was extremely dense. **Modern astronomers** only identified this dense companion, Sirius B, in 1970, so how was it that this remote African tribe had known of it? The puzzle prompted Robert Temple to speculate, in his book *The Sirius Mystery*, that the Dogon must have been visited by **extraterrestrials** from Sirius.

12 Soukous

The variety of **Congolese music** called *soukous*, with its high-tempo beat, thumping bass lines and ringing guitars, is among the most popular - and sexy - of Africa's many musical styles. *Soukous* has its roots in Cuban music, particularly rumba, which became popular in the booming cities of Leopoldville (now Kinshasa) and Brazzaville during the early 1940s. For a time the indigenous music industry boomed, but these days, with the average Congolese income at less than US$1 a day and music often being sold on bootlegged cassettes, the stars of *soukous* are making most of their money in the West.

While many classic recordings are unavailable on CD, there are plenty of **compilations** to get you started on Congolese music, including the CDs *Rough Guide to Congolese Soukous* and *Rough Guide to Franco*.

Five Legendary Congolese musicians

Papa Wendo The first star of African rumba.

Joseph Kabasele Leader of African Jazz, one of the big bands that transformed the African take on Cuban rumba into *soukous*.

Franco Luambo Nicknamed the "Sorcerer of the Guitar", Franco was front man of OK Jazz, African Jazz's big rival during the 1950s.

Tabu Ley Rochereau His band African Fiesta dominated Congolese music in the 1960s.

Papa Wemba The best-known *soukous* musician around today.

13 Hot spots

Africa holds two records for extreme **heat**. The highest temperature ever recorded was in the Libyan town of Al 'Aziziyah where, on September 13, 1922, the mercury reached 57.7°C (135.9°F). The town with the highest mean temperature is Dakol, Ethiopia, with an average daily temperature of nearly 34.5°C (94°F).

14. Despots and democracy

Since achieving their **independence**, most countries in Africa have suffered from some sort of "democratic deficit" – ruthless dictators, flawed elections, bloody coups d'etat. There have been some success stories, however, such as when South Africans flocked to the polls in 1994 to elect Nelson Mandela and the ANC. Another less heralded but equally important moment was in 2005, when Liberia's Ellen Johnson-Sirleaf became Africa's first elected **female leader**, defeating soccer legend George Weah in the vote.

"I am the hero of Africa."

Idi Amin (Ugandan dictator)

15. The "Big Five"

Much of the talk on an African safari is about spotting lions, elephants, buffaloes, rhinoceroses and leopards – collectively the "Big Five". The term has nothing to do with size, beauty or rarity, but was in fact coined by game hunters to refer to the five most challenging animals to track down and kill.

He who waits until the whole animal is visible spears its tail.

Swahili proverb

16 African explorers

The colourful exploits of European adventurers such as David Livingston, Mungo Park and Richard Burton are well known, but arguably the world's greatest explorer is actually from Africa. In the fourteenth century, Morocco's Ibn Battuta travelled over 100,000km a over a thirty-year period. In addition to North, East and West Africa, Battutu claimed to have been all over the Middle East, Central, East and Southeast Asia and China, far outstripping the travelling credentials of his near-contemporary, Marco Polo.

17 Good food

Africa's main staples are cassava, maize, millet, rice, sorghum, plantains and yams. Among the more distinctive is *teff*, found only in Ethiopia and Eritrea. It's used to make *injera*, a crêpe-like, faintly sourish flat bread; tear off pieces of *injera* with your hands and use it to scoop up the spicy stews served alongside.

"Mount Kenya used to be sacred to the Kikuyu people. If the mountain was still given the reverence the culture accorded it, people would not have allowed illegal logging and clear-cutting in the forests. Cultural revival might be the only thing that stands between the conservation or destruction of the environment."

Wangari Maathai, Kenyan environmentalist and winner of the 2004 Nobel Peace Prize

18 Beliefs

A wide range of **indigenous beliefs** co-exist with Africa's two main faiths, **Christianity** and **Islam**. Traditionally, for example, the Ibo of Nigeria believe that every man has two souls. Upon death, the life force perishes with the body, but the eternal ego survives in the form of a ghost, a shadow or a reflection. The spirit of a good Ibo will come back as something like a cow, leopard or elephant; a bad person might return as something like a plant.

19 Islands

Continental Africa is surrounded by six **island nations**. The Atlantic has Cape Verde, and São Tomé and Príncipe; both are Portuguese-speaking. In the Indian Ocean are Madagascar (the world's fourth largest island), Mauritius, the Comoros and the Seychelles. Mauritius is among Africa's richest countries, in per capita terms – it's on a par with South Africa.

20 War

Most African countries have suffered some sort of **violent internal strife** since winning their independence. The fighting in the Democratic Republic of the Congo has claimed over four million lives, making it the deadliest conflict since World War II. In 1994, it took just one hundred days for some 800,000 Tutsi and Hutu civilians to be slaughtered during the Rwandan genocide. Nearly two million people have been displaced because of the fighting in Sudan. Africa's longest civil war, in Angola, lasted sixteen years.

"If you want to make peace with your enemy, you have to work with your enemy. Then he becomes your partner."

Nelson Mandela

21 Five festivals & events

Africa's festivals are incredibly diverse, rooted in religion or traditional customs, celebrating the continent's achievements, or staged in the interest of sport or simply for fun.

FESTIVAL/EVENT	WHEN/WHERE	WHAT HAPPENS
Dakar Rally	January, in Europe and North and West Africa	Once the Paris–Dakar Rally, this epic race is now conducted along a variety of routes, ranging as far afield as Egypt
Voodoo Day	January 10 in Ouidah, Benin	Voodoo followers from all over the world come to perform ceremonies and make offerings of sacrificial animals
International Camel Derby and Festival	August, in Maralal, Kenya	Professional camel racing, pitting Kenya's finest against international competition
Imilchil Festival	September, in Imilchil, Morocco	Men and women from Berber tribes traditionally gather in Imilchil to get married, twenty couples at a time
Festival Panafricain du Cinéma (Fespaco)	February of odd-numbered years, in Ouagadougou, Burkina Faso	A major celebration of African film-making, attracting thousands

22 Language

There are four main language families in Africa. The vast majority of Africans speak tongues belonging to the **Afro-Asiatic**, **Niger-Congo** and **Nilo-Saharan** families. The languages that comprise the Khoisan family, meanwhile, are virtually extinct, spoken by only a few thousand people in southwestern Africa. Khoisan languages are known for their use of clicks, consonants consisting of various clicking and popping sounds produced by the teeth, tongue and palate.

23 Street names

In the fight by black Africans to rid themselves of colonial powers or white oppression, a few individuals stand out, their achievements commemorated in street names. There are hundreds of **Nelson Mandela** streets, avenues and boulevards all across Africa. Other popular independence leaders immortalized by an address include **Patrice Lumumba** of the Democratic Repulic of Congo, **Kwame Nkrumah** of Ghana and **Julius Nyerere** of Tanzania.

"If you are in hiding, don't light a fire."

Ghanaian proverb

24 Deserts

Africa is home to three deserts, which together take up more than a quarter of the continent's area. The **Sahara**, covering much of Africa north of the equator, is the largest desert in the world, and creeping desertification means that it is constantly encroaching on the Sahel, the strip of land separating the desert from the savanna. The **Namib** in Namibia has been around for at least 80 million years, making it the world's oldest desert. Finally, the **Kalahari** in southern Africa is relatively well vegetated thanks to occasional rainfall.

25 Alcohol

In rural parts of many African countries, a kind of **wine** is made by collecting the sap of palm trees and leaving it to ferment briefly. After just a few hours, the result is a very sweet tipple, one which can become quite potent if fermentation continues for a day or more. A sort of beer is also produced by brewing millet, sometimes with herbs and spices. Give a wide berth to any moonshine that you may come across, however, as spirits can be dangerously adulterated.

"The darkest thing about Africa has always been our ignorance of it."

George Kimble (geographer)

25 Ultimate experiences Africa small print

ROUGH GUIDES – don't just travel

We hope you've been inspired by the experiences in this book. To us, they sum up what makes Africa such an extraordinary and stimulating place to travel. There are 24 other books in the 25 Ultimate Experiences series, each conceived to whet your appetite for travel and for everything the world has to offer. As well as covering the globe, the 25s series also includes books on **Journeys, World Food, Adventure Travel, Places to Stay, Ethical Travel, Wildlife Adventures** and **Wonders of the World**.

When you start planning your trip, Rough Guides' new-look guides, maps and phrasebooks are the ultimate companions. For 25 years we've been refining what makes a good guidebook and we now include more colour photos and more information – on average 50% more pages – than any of our competitors. Just look for the sky-blue spines.

Rough Guides don't just travel – we also believe in getting the most out of life without a passport. Since the publication of the bestselling Rough Guides to **The Internet** and **World Music**, we've brought out a wide range of lively and authoritative guides on everything from **Climate Change** to **Hip-Hop**, from **MySpace** to **Film Noir** and from **The Brain** to **The Rolling Stones**.

Publishing information

Rough Guide 25 Ultimate experiences Africa Published May 2007 by Rough Guides Ltd, 80 Strand, London WC2R 0RL
345 Hudson St, 4th Floor,
New York, NY 10014, USA
14 Local Shopping Centre, Panchsheel Park, New Delhi 110017, India
Distributed by the Penguin Group
Penguin Books Ltd,
80 Strand, London WC2R 0RL
Penguin Group (USA)
375 Hudson Street, NY 10014, USA
Penguin Group (Australia)
250 Camberwell Road, Camberwell, Victoria 3124, Australia
Penguin Books Canada Ltd,
10 Alcorn Avenue, Toronto, Ontario, Canada M4V 1E4
Penguin Group (NZ)
67 Apollo Drive, Mairangi Bay, Auckland 1310, New Zealand
Printed in China

80pp
A catalogue record for this book is available from the British Library
ISBN: 978-1-84353-838-7

1 3 5 7 9 8 6 4 2

Rough Guide credits

Editor: Richard Lim
Design & picture research: Coralie Bickford-Smith, Samantha Johnson
Cartography: Maxine Repath, Katie Lloyd-Jones
Cover design: Diana Jarvis, Chloë Roberts
Production: Aimee Hampson, Katherine Owers
Proofreader: James Smart

The authors

Miranda Davies (Experience 15) is a writer and editor with a passion for West African music. **Jens Finke** (Experience 19) is the author of Rough Guides' *First-Time Africa*, as well as Rough Guides to Tanzania and to Zanzibar. **Emma Gregg** (Experiences 1, 9, 11, 12, 13, 22) is editor of *Travel Africa* magazine, and co-author of the *Rough Guide to The Gambia*. **Daniel Jacobs** (Experiences 4, 10, 16, 24) is the co-author of Rough Guides to Morocco and Tunisia. **Donald Reid** (Experiences 3, 17) has lived in Cape Town and is co-author of the *Rough Guide to South Africa, Lesotho and Swaziland*. **Chris Scott** (Experience 20) has authored books and DVDs on overlanding through the Sahara. **Henry Stedman** (Experience 8) is the author of a bestselling guide to Kilimanjaro and has climbed the mountain more than half-a-dozen times. **Richard Trillo** (Experiences 2, 6, 14, 18, 21, 23, 25) has authored Rough Guides to Kenya, West Africa and The Gambia. **Ross Velton** (Experience 7, Miscellany) has written Bradt guides to Mali and Mozambique, and is co-author of the *Rough Guide to Florida*. **Beth Wooldridge** (Experience 5) has lived in Ethiopia while working for the UK charity VSO.

Picture credits

Cover Giraffes at Amboseli National Park, Kilimanjaro © SIME/Schmid Reinhard/ 4corners images
2 Tourists ride elephants in the Okavango Delta © Louise Gubb/Corbis Saba
6 Marrakesh market © Peter Adams/Alamy
8–9 Tourists ride elephants in the Okavango Delta © Louise Gubb/Corbis Saba
10–11 Two Maasai watch a hot-air balloon flight © Nigel Pavitt/John-Warburton-Lee
12–13 Pony-trekking in Lesotho © Buddy Mays/Corbis
14–15 Stall selling dried fruit, Fes © Helene Roberts/Alamy
16–17 Reading the Bible in a rock church © Kazuyoshi Nomachi/Corbis
18–19 Youssou N'Dour © Nic Bothma/epa/ Corbis
20–21 Mozambique coastline © Robert Harding Picture Library/Alamy
22–23 Mount Kilimanjaro at sunrise © David Poole/Robert Harding
24–25 Aerial view of Victoria Falls © Geoff Renner/Robert Harding Picture Library
26–27 Underground dwellings at Matmata © Frans Lemmens/Getty Images
28–29 Winemaker checking wine, Stellenbosch © Alain Proust/Cephas Picture Library/Alamy; Champagne maturing in bottles © John Warburton-Lee
30–31 Baby mountain gorilla © Joe McDonald/Corbis
32–33 Dogon huts © Jose Azal/Getty Images
34–35 Wikki Warm Springs © Gary Cook/ Alamy
36–37 Festival in the Desert © Suzanne Porter
38–39 Theatre at Leptis Magna © Roger Wood/Corbis
40–41 Cape buffalo © Paul Allen/Robert Harding; hippos yawning © Anne & Steve Toon/Robert Harding Picture Library
42–43 Printing cloth, Kumasi © David C. Poole/Robert Harding; fishing pirogues on Cape Coast beach © Ariadne Van Zandbergen/Getty Images; St George's Castle © Jenny Pate/Robert Harding Picture Library
44–45 Wildlife-spotting in the Ngorongoro Crater © Keith Drew
46–47 Saharan rock formation © Kazuyoshi Nomachi/Corbis
48–49 Riverbank flowers © Martin Harvey/ Gallo Images/Corbis
50–51 Desert chameleon, Skeleton Coast © Pete Oxford/Robert Harding Picture Library
52–53 Volcanic caldera, Boavista © Robert Van Der Hilst/Corbis; Satellite view of Cape Verde © InterNetwork Media/Getty Images
54–55 Jemaa el Fna overview © Robert Frerck/Getty Images; Jemaa el Fna at dusk © Sergio Pitamitz/cefa/Corbis; Dried-fruit stall © Samantha Johnson; Marrakesh market © Peter Adams/Alamy; Chefs preparing food © Neil Emmerson/ Robert Harding Picture Library
56–57 Lamu Town © Nigel Pavitt/John Warburton-Lee
58 Reading the Bible in a rock church © Kazuyoshi Nomachi/Corbis
72 Two Maasai watch a hot-air balloon flight © Nigel Pavitt/John-Warburton-Lee

ROUGH GUIDES
Australia
ROUGH GUIDES
Cuba
ROUGH GUIDES
Britain
ROUGH GUIDES
Singapore
ROUGH GUIDES
Vietnam
ROUGH GUIDES
New York City

Index